FREE DVD

Essential Test Tips DVD from Trivium Test Prep

Dear Customer,

Thank you for purchasing from Cirrus Test Prep! Whether you're looking to join the military, get into college, or advance your career, we're honored to be a part of your journey.

To show our appreciation (and to help you relieve a little of that test-prep stress), we're offering a **FREE *MTEL Essential Test Tips DVD**** by Cirrus Test Prep. Our DVD includes 35 test preparation strategies that will help keep you calm and collected before and during your big exam. All we ask is that you email us your feedback and describe your experience with our product. Amazing, awful, or just so-so: we want to hear what you have to say!

To receive your **FREE *MTEL Essential Test Tips DVD***, please email us at 5star@cirrustestprep.com. Include "Free 5 Star" in the subject line and the following information in your email:

1. The title of the product you purchased.
2. Your rating from 1 – 5 (with 5 being the best).
3. Your feedback about the product, including how our materials helped you meet your goals and ways in which we can improve our products.
4. Your full name and shipping address so we can send your **FREE *MTEL Essential Test Tips DVD***.

If you have any questions or concerns please feel free to contact us directly at 5star@cirrustestprep.com. Thank you, and good luck with your studies!

* Please note that the free DVD is not included with this book. To receive the free DVD, please follow the instructions above.

MTEL English as a Second Language (54) Flash Cards

Test Prep Review with 300+ Flash Cards for the MTEL ESL Exam

Introduction

Congratulations on choosing to take the Massachusetts Tests for Educator Licensure (MTEL) English as a Second Language (ESL) (54) exam! By purchasing this book, you've taken the first step toward becoming an ESL teacher.

This guide will provide you with a detailed overview of the MTEL, so you know exactly what to expect on test day. We'll take you through all the concepts covered on the test and give you the opportunity to test your knowledge with practice questions. Even if it's been a while since you last took a major test, don't worry; we'll make sure you're more than ready!

What is the MTEL?

MTEL tests are a part of teaching licensure in Massachusetts. Along with the MTEL communication and literacy skills test, passing an MTEL subject test is a part of a prospective teacher's application for licensure. These tests are criterion referenced and standardized to measure your skills and knowledge in English as a Second Language. For more information about credentialing in Massachusetts, refer to the MTEL website.

What's on the MTEL?

The MTEL ESL test gauges your second-language instruction and learning. Four hours is allotted for the entirety of the test; you may complete test sections in any order. You will be asked to answer 100 multiple-choice questions and two open-response questions. The multiple-choice questions will be both application and fact based. In the open-response section, you will provide written responses to assignments that ask you to evaluate an ESL student's work. Each answer should be 150 – 300 words (one to two pages). Your response will be evaluated on its adherence to the topic presented, demonstrated understanding of the subject, use of supporting evidence, and soundness of argument. Be sure to keep your audience (other educational professionals) in mind!

MTEL ESL (54) Exam

Type of Question	Subject	Approximate Number of Questions	Approximate Percentage
Multiple Choice	Foundations of Second-Language Instruction	44	35%
	Second-Language and Content Learning	56	45%
Open Response	Integration of Knowledge and Understanding	2	20%
Total		100 (and 2 open response)	4 hours

You will answer approximately forty-four questions (35 percent of the entire test) on the foundations of second-language instruction. This section will test your knowledge of instruction for English language learners (ELL) and basic sociolinguistic and linguistic concepts. You will be expected to understand the development of second-language acquisition, the processes through which second languages are acquired from first languages, and the variations that can affect the process of language acquisition. Approaches and best practices regarding ELLs' language development will also be covered in this section.

You will answer approximately fifty-six questions (45 percent of the test) on second-language and content learning. The role of aural, oral, writing, and reading instruction and assessment tools in ESL programs as well as how those assessments can be used to plan and adjust classroom instruction will be covered in this section. Be aware of the shortcomings of assessment methods in evaluating ELLs. This section also tests your knowledge of diverse learners and ability to apply pedagogy in order to reach learners of different backgrounds and needs. As an ESL teacher, you will be expected to create a learning environment that is effective for a multicultural and multilingual student population.

HOW IS THE MTEL SCORED?

On the MTEL, the number of correctly answered questions is used to create your scaled score. The multiple-choice questions consist of 80 percent of your overall score, while the open-response questions comprise the other 20 percent. Scores are scaled to a number in the range of 100 – 300, a passing score being 240. The score shows your performance on the test as a whole and is scaled to allow comparison across various versions of the test. There is no penalty for guessing on the MTEL, so be sure to eliminate answer choices and answer every question. If you still do not know the answer, guess; you may get it right! Keep in mind that some multiple-choice questions are experimental questions for the purpose of the MTEL test makers and will not count toward your overall score. However, since those questions are not indicated on the test, you must respond to every question.

Scores are reported three to four weeks after testing on your online account. Your score report indicates whether you passed and your general performance in each subarea of the test. For more information about scoring, refer to http://www.mtel.nesinc.com/.

HOW IS THE MTEL ADMINISTERED?

The MTEL is administered continuously year round at testing centers located throughout Massachusetts and across the nation. To register for a test and find a testing site near you, go to http://www.mtel.nesinc.com/. At this site, you can create an MTEL account, check testing appointment times, and find instructions for registering. The MTEL is administered as a computerized test, and the website offers computer-based testing tutorials so that you can become acclimated to that format.

On the day of your test, be sure to bring your admission ticket (which is provided when you register) and photo ID. The testing facility will provide an area outside of the testing room to store your personal belongings. You are allowed no personal effects in the testing area. Cell phones and other electronic, photographic, recording, or listening devices are not permitted in the testing center at all, and bringing those items may be cause for dismissal, forfeiture of your testing fees, and cancellation of your scores. For details on what is and is not permitted at your testing center, refer to the MTEL website.

About Cirrus Test Prep

Cirrus Test Prep study guides are designed by current and former educators and are tailored to meet your needs as an incoming educator. Our guides offer all of the resources necessary to help you pass teacher certification tests across the nation.

Cirrus clouds are graceful, wispy clouds characterized by their high altitude. Just like cirrus clouds, Cirrus Test Prep's goal is to help educators "aim high" when it comes to obtaining their teacher certification and entering the classroom.

About This Guide

This guide will help you master the most important test topics and also develop critical test-taking skills. We have built features into our books to prepare you for your tests and increase your score. Along with a detailed summary of the test's format, content, and scoring, we offer an in-depth overview of the content knowledge required to pass the test. Our sidebars provide interesting information, highlight key concepts, and review content so that you can solidify your understanding of the exam's concepts. Test your knowledge with sample questions and detailed answer explanations in the text that help you think through exam problems, as well as with practice tests that reflect the content and format of the MTEL. We're pleased you've chosen Cirrus to be a part of your professional journey.

intonation

morpheme

Abraham Maslow

the way the voice rises and falls in speech

the smallest unit of meaning in a language

developed the hierarchy of needs, which he theorized to be the unconscious desires that motivate people

subordinating conjunction

stereotype

voiceless sounds

joins a dependent clause to an independent clause to which it is related

an oversimplified belief that all people from a certain group or with certain characteristics are the same

sounds made without vibrating the vocal chords

Howard Gardner

classroom management

independent (or main) clause

created the theory of multiple intelligences; proposed that using a person's area of giftedness to demonstrate intellect will help learners achieve their potential

active management of the physical classroom space, the culture of the classroom, and individual student behavior

a clause that can stand alone as its own sentence

one-word stage

verbs

reclassification criteria

stage of language acquisition; characterized by a child's use of a single word to convey a full meaning

express action (*run*, *jump*, *play*) or state of being (*is*, *seems*)

used to determine when English learners have achieved the language skills necessary to succeed in English-only classrooms

humor stage

SIFE

grade-equivalent

stage of acculturation; when students start to come to terms with their circumstances and move toward acceptance of their new culture

Students with Interrupted Formal Education

score found using the average score of students who fall into that grade

labial consonant sound

gerund phrase

connotation

sound produced by the top and bottom lips coming together (*m*)

phrase that begins with a gerund (verbs that end in –*ing* and act as nouns)

the emotional association of a word

helping verb

Woodcock-Muñoz Language Survey

audio-lingual method (ALM)

verb that indicates tense (when the action occurred)

an individually administered assessment that measures cognitive aspects of language proficiency in the form of vocabulary usage, verbal analogies, and letter-word identification

an oral-based approach to language instruction developed by linguists and behavioral psychologists; teaches the target language through repetition

English Language Proficiency Assessment for the 21st Century

phonetics

silent way

consortium of states whose assessments are aligned to the English Language Proficiency standards developed by the Council of Chief State School Officers (CCSSO), which determines the states' college- and career-ready (CCR) standards

the study of the production of sounds in speech

teaching method based on the idea that language learning should be much like problem-solving and discovery learning; teachers are as silent as possible during lessons in order to promote student participation and experimentation and to concentrate on learning over teaching

age-equivalent score

dependent (or subordinate) clause

inferential item

found using the average score of students within an age group

a clause that cannot stand alone as its own sentence

a piece of information that requires the test taker to read between the lines in order to determine what an author is implying

communicative competence

two-word stage

early stage of literacy development

the ability to speak a language both appropriately in a social context as well as correctly in terms of rules and structure

stage of language acquisition; children begin to learn words and use word combinations

characterized by the learner's use of multiple strategies to predict and understand words

lead and support

intermediate fluency

free morpheme

teaching strategy that relies on one instructor assuming a lead teaching role with the other providing support as needed

fourth stage of second-language acquisition; learners have acquired a vocabulary of about 6,000 words and are able to speak in more complex sentences and correct many of their own errors

a morpheme that can stand on its own

literal item

semicolon

monitor hypothesis

information that refers directly back to the content of the reading material where the answer is defined word by word

punctuation used to join two closely related sentences that could each stand on their own

knowledge that is gained through formal learning that can be used to monitor speech but is not useful in spontaneous speech

validity

scaffold

positive behavioral support

indicates how well an assessment measures what it is intended to measure; a test is not considered valid if it is not reliable

the support that allows a child to work above their independent level and is gradually removed as the learner gains mastery

a social learning approach that assumes all persistent behavior choices are logical, so a persistent misbehavior must serve some purpose

Cognitive Academic Language Proficiency (CALP)

natural order hypothesis

Sapir-Whorf hypothesis

language needed for academic work and study

one of the five hypotheses of the monitor model; posits that language is attained in a foreseeable pattern by all learners

proposition that a person's thoughts and actions are determined by the language(s) that person speaks

classic conditioning

assimilation

passive voice

learning a response to stimuli or the environment

when a speech sound changes due to the influence of nearby sounds

a sentence construction in which the subject of the sentence is receiving the action of the main verb

language policy

Basic Interpersonal Communication Skills (BICS)

norm referenced

the set of actions a government takes to regulate what language(s) is/are spoken in the given country

social skills students use in everyday life when socializing on the playground, in the cafeteria, and outside of school

a test that measures students in comparison with other students of the same age

integrative services

Lau v. Nichols

total physical response (TPR)

a system where all agencies are working in cooperation, and the clients—ELLs and their families—have access to a streamlined and connected range of needed assistance

This 1974 Supreme Court ruled that the San Francisco Unified School District had denied Chinese-speaking students' rights to equal educational opportunities; the ruling stated that schools receiving federal funds must provide programs to address the language needs of non-English-speaking students.

an instructional method that provides students, particularly beginning language learners, with the opportunity to acquire language skills by listening to and following spoken commands

bound morpheme

sociolinguistics

individualist culture

a morpheme that must be attached to a word to have meaning

the study of language and its relation to society and culture

characterized by the value placed on the individual and individual accomplishments, rather than on the family or group to which the individual belongs

sheltered instruction

collectivist culture

Keyes v. School District No. 1, Denver, Colorado

provides English language learners with access to appropriate, grade-level content while supporting their need for ongoing language instruction

prioritizes the needs and outcomes of groups such as the greater community, society, or nation

The 1973 Supreme Court decision ruled in favor of the plaintiffs, giving Latino students the same rights ascribed to desegregation as had only previously been given to African American students.

standards-based education

infinitive phrase

extrinsic motivation

education based on a set of learning outcomes clearly set by the district and state that all students are expected to achieve

a verbal phrase that may act as a noun, an adjective, or an adverb

motivation driven by external rewards

English Language Proficiency (ELP) standards

discourse competence

linguistics

identify the target language development skills an English learner is expected to meet in the context of instruction that is appropriately scaffolded for optimal learning

the ability to effectively arrange smaller units of language like phrases and sentences into cohesive works like letters, speeches, conversations, and articles

the scientific study of language

clause

relative pronoun

ESL paraprofessional

contains both a subject and a predicate

a pronoun that begins a dependent clause (*I live in Texas, which is a large state.*)

an education professional whose role is to assist ESL teachers and ELL students

utterances

conference

indirect teaching

speech acts of one or more words that contain a single idea and are surrounded on both sides by silence

a meeting between teacher and student in which learning is orally assessed and evaluated

student-centered instruction in which the teacher facilitates opportunities for students to construct their own learning

linguistic relativism

WIDA

thematic unit

the belief that language only partially influences human thought and action

a consortium of states that promotes research, standards, and professional development to support ELLs in academics and language learning

integrating curricula across content areas under a general theme

antecedent

cultural norms

phrase

the noun a pronoun replaces

the rules and standards a group uses to determine what are appropriate or inappropriate, expected, and accepted behaviors

a group of words that communicates a partial idea and lacks either a subject or a predicate

cloze procedure

differentiation

induction

the practice of omitting words from the text as a reading comprehension activity

providing curriculum for students based on their individual needs, including learning styles and level

process by which learners figure out the rules of the language as they acquire speaking and listening skills, learning through a combined process of imitation and trial and error

listening guides

Language Experience Approach (LEA)

cooperative learning

statements or questions that provide instructional focus when listening to a lecture or other form of auditory instruction

uses learners' prior knowledge and experiences to generate specific lessons that are designed to enhance the learning of each individual student

when the teacher places students into small groups and gives them a task to complete together

discovery learning

diagnostic assessment

cognates

when students perform experiments or research information to comprehend new concepts

given before a learning experience to measure the students' baseline knowledge

visually similar words

schema

underextension

strategic competence

the framework of understanding in a child's brain

when a child's definition of a word is too narrow

the ability to recognize and repair breakdowns in communication through strategic planning and/or redirecting

guided practice

period

appositive phrase

practicing a new concept with scaffolded support from the teacher

punctuation used to end imperative and declarative sentences

a particular type of noun phrase that renames the word or group of words that precedes it

cultural awareness

FANBOYS

preposition

the development of sensitivity to and understanding of other cultures and the ways culture influences individuals

the coordinating conjunctions: For, And, Nor, But, Or, Yet, So

sets up relationships in time (*after the party*) or space (*under the cushions*) within a sentence

English-language learner (ELL)

monochronic cultures

Family Educational Rights and Privacy Act of 1974 (FERPA)

student whose native language is not English

culture in which time is seen as linear, with one event happening at a time

federal law that prohibits schools from sharing identifiable information about students

formative assessment

self-actualization

inflectional morphemes

informal assessments that are used throughout the learning experiences to help teachers make instructional decisions and to provide feedback to students

the final state in Maslow's hierarchy of needs; the individual has realized their potential and seeks fulfillment and growth

bound morphemes that do not greatly alter a word's meaning or part of speech

behaviorist theory

World Englishes

cultural bias

suggests that repeated exposure to stimuli can create learning: the more frequently a behavior is performed, the more quickly it will become habit

localized varieties of English, particularly those that have developed in territories under the influence of the United Kingdom or the United States

occurs when a test offends or penalizes a test taker due to items related to socioeconomic status, gender, or ethnicity

gerund

fluency stage

push-in ESOL programs

noun that is formed by adding –*ing* to a verb

stage of literacy development; characterized by the ability to maintain meaning throughout longer and more complex texts

when ESOL teachers travel to content classrooms, providing additional support and services to language learners; intended to maximize the time English language learners spend in general education content classrooms

Edward Thorndike

epenthesis

conjunction

researcher whose work initially led to operant conditioning; Thorndike's learning laws include the law of effect, the law of readiness, and the law of exercise

inserting an additional sound in the middle of a word

short word that connects words, phrases, or sentences

Lawrence Kohlberg

emergent literacy stage

cognitive process

identified the stages of moral development

stage of literacy development; the competencies that are developed in early childhood and preschool

acquisition of new knowledge and skills and the ability to apply new learning to new situations and draw conclusions from it

preoperational stage

hostility stage

improper noun

second stage of Piaget's cognitive-developmental theory; two to seven years of age; a child's intelligence is progressively demonstrated through his or her use of symbols

stage of acculturation; students are getting comfortable with getting around and meeting basic needs, but they may feel at odds with the new culture and may be homesick

a general person, place, thing, or idea

concrete operational stage

interrogative pronoun

input hypothesis

third stage of Piaget's cognitive-developmental theory; seven to eleven years of age; children demonstrate increased intelligence through logical and organized methods of thinking

a pronoun that begins a question and requests information about people, places, things, ideas, location, time, means, and purposes (*What is your favorite color?*)

one of the five hypotheses of the monitor model; states that comprehensible input is necessary for students who are in the process of acquiring a new language

pronoun

voicing

advanced fluency

takes the place of a noun in order to minimize repetition

when a voiceless consonant changes to a voiced consonant because of nearby sounds

fifth stage of second-language acquisition; learners have achieved cognitive language proficiency in their learned language; they demonstrate near-native ability and use complex, multiphrase and multiclause sentences to convey their ideas

standardized test

verb phrase

connected speech

a test administered to all students in a consistent way and then graded in the same way so that score comparisons may be accurately made

composed of the main verb along with its helping verbs

when speakers simplify sounds and run words together

speech therapist

Language Assessment Scales (LAS)

preproduction

a certified professional who diagnoses and treats communication disorders

designed to measure the oral proficiency and reading and writing abilities of K – 12 students; measure content such as vocabulary, listening comprehension, and story retelling and are available in both English and Spanish

first stage of second-language acquisition; learners may refrain from speaking but will listen and may copy words down and respond to visual cues

end mark

Every Student Succeeds Act (ESSA)

language modeling

punctuation used at the end of a sentence

replaced the No Child Left Behind Act(NCLB); deemphasized standardized testing for English language learners

providing accurate examples of speech and language for language learners

register

communicative approach

intrinsic motivation

a variety of a language used in a particular setting

a combination of several methods of language instruction based on the notion that successful language acquisition comes from the need to communicate real meaning

one's personal drive to succeed or learn

Americans with Disabilities Act (ADA)

complex sentence

sensorimotor stage

prohibits discrimination based on disabilities; in schools, this includes activities that take place both on and off campus, including athletics and extracurricular activities

has only one independent clause and one or more dependent clauses

first stage of Piaget's cognitive-developmental theory; birth to two years of age; a child's knowledge is based upon physical interactions and experiences

remediation

positive transfer

compound-complex sentence

the additional support provided to regular education students to bridge gaps in learning

when students find similarities between their native language and English and use those similarities to aid in their learning

has two or more independent clauses and one or more dependent clause

determiner

morpheme acquisition order

poverty of stimulus

the articles *a*, *an*, and *the*

the pattern in which morphemes are learned as people acquire language

assertion by Noam Chomsky that children are not born with enough exposure to their native languages to explain their ability to understand phonemes, and therefore this exposure cannot account for the sum of their learned language

connectionism

adverb

grapheme

holds that language comprehension and production abilities develop through continual engagement with language

word that describes or modifies verbs, adjectives, and other adverbs

symbol used to represent phonemes

lesson planning

early production stage

home language survey

the alignment of standards, assessments, and learning materials to create a learning trajectory for a course of instruction

second stage of second-language acquisition; learners achieve a 1,000-word receptive and active vocabulary and can produce single-word and two- to three-word phrases

short form that is sent home as part of a school enrollment packet; used by school districts to determine the primary languages spoken in students' homes

transfer

verbal prompting

place of articulation

applying knowledge of a first language to another; can be both positive and negative

using words or beginning phonemes to assist students

the point where two speech organs come together to make a sound

summative assessment

reinforcement

interdisciplinary unit

formal or informal assessments that evaluate student achievement after learning takes place

the process of strengthening behavior through rewards or consequences

a unit of study in which content from all subject areas is integrated

authentic materials

productive language skills

home stage

materials intended for use by native language speakers and not second-language learners

abilities related to producing comprehensible language from within, such as in writing and speaking tasks

stage of acculturation; students are comfortable within their new culture and embrace it as home

receptive language skills

adverb clause

interjection

abilities related to understanding language that is received from an external source, such as oral directions and commentary, visuals, sounds, and written words

a dependent clause that modifies a verb, adjective, or adverb in the main or independent clause of a sentence

word that express emotion, such as *oh* and *wow*

derivational morpheme

whole language approach

transitive verb

morpheme that creates a word that has a new meaning or part of speech

the idea that learners should start at the top and work their way down, meaning that language should be considered in its complete form prior to being broken down into smaller pieces

verb that requires a direct object

voiced sound

standard conventions of written English

assertive discipline

sound made by vibrating the vocal chords

the grammar, usage, and mechanics rules that govern the proper production of the English language, particularly in written form

a classroom management technique in which the teacher takes clear control over the classroom and its dynamics

individualized education plan (IEP)

No Child Left Behind Act of 2001 (NCLB)

interlanguage

an annual meeting for each special education student that outlines the student's learning goals and identifies the accommodations and modifications that will be offered to the student

Title III of NCLB required that LEP students be placed in a language instruction education program, and it defined what constitutes a language program.

the learner's present understanding of the language he or she is learning; a rule-based system that blends aspects of the learner's first language with those of the second

discrete language skills

transformational grammar

task-based instruction (TBI)

aspects of language that are governed by rules such as phonics, grammar, and syntax

revolutionized the study of language by turning the focus away from semiotics and meaning, toward the system of rules that dictate proper sentence construction

lessons are designed around the completion of tasks that are either assigned by instructors or selected by students; tasks are usually defined as activities that are carried out by learners using their language knowledge and resources

constructivism

false cognates

syntax

when students construct their own knowledge through learning experiences

words that appear similar but are different in meaning

how words are arranged into phrases and sentences

correlative conjunction

task analysis

Annual Measurable Achievement Objectives (AMAOs)

whether/or, either/or, neither/nor, both/and, not only/but also; functions like a coordinating conjunction

the teacher takes a larger, complex goal and breaks it down into smaller, concrete components that lead to the ultimate goal

objectives required for school districts to receive Title III funds: 1) increase the number or percentage of ELLs *progressing* toward proficiency in English; 2) increase the number or percentage of ELLs *reaching* proficiency in English; and 3) ELLs must make adequate yearly progress (AYP) toward content knowledge

divergent questions

convergent questions

code-switching

open-ended questions designed to assess a student's ability to analyze, evaluate, and create

questions that have a clear, correct answer

mixing words from a first language in with the language being learned

phonemic awareness

MODEL

mechanics

the knowledge that words are made of specific sounds

Measure of Developing English Language; series of assessments that educators can use to identify and place English learners as well as to monitor their progress toward instructional goals

the rules of print that do not exist in spoken language, including spelling, capitalization, punctuation, and proper paragraphing

pidgin

Common Core Standards

active listening

a grammatically simplified mode of communicating that uses elements of two or more languages

the predominant set of standards used across most states for math and English language arts

improves listening skills by structuring how a person listens and responds to the person who is talking

authentic language

Equal Educational Opportunities Act of 1974 (EEOA)

aspiration

reading materials from books, newspapers, the internet, and other real-life sources

states that that no state shall deny the access to equal education by "failing to take appropriate action to overcome language barriers that impede equal participation by its students in its educational programs"

sound produced with a burst of air out of the mouth (*h*)

universal grammar

linguistic set

affix

Noam Chomsky's theory that children are born with the innate ability to understand the human voice and to distinguish between different parts of language

a group of words and rules that compose an individual's working knowledge of a language

a bound morpheme that can be added to a root word to change its meaning, grammatical function, tense, case, or gender

subject

language bias

curriculum-based measures

what a sentence is about; includes the noun that is performing the main action of the sentence and the noun's modifiers

occurs when a test that was originally developed for use in one language is translated to and administered in another language

determine student progress and performance based on specific lessons presented in the unit

team teaching

B.F. Skinner

pre-speech stage

content area and ESL teachers take an equal role in teaching all the students in a content classroom

expanded on operant conditioning, but focused on responding to environment in lieu of responding to stimuli

stage of language acquisition; infants learn to pay attention to speech, inflection, and rhythm before they begin to speak

speech emergence

accommodation

polychronic culture

third stage of second-language acquisition; learners are able to chunk simple words and phrases into sentences that may or may not be grammatically correct

provide a student access to the same curriculum as their grade-level peers, but information is presented in a different way

culture that views time more holistically and is able to conceive of many things happening at once

exclamation point

content-based language instruction

acculturation

used at the end of interjections or exclamations

the use of subject matter material (such as math, science, or social studies) as the basis for practicing communicative skills

the process of adapting to a new culture

noun

idiom

reciprocal determinism

names a person, place, thing, or idea

a group of words whose meaning cannot be deduced from the meanings of the individual words in the group

the theory by Albert Bandura that behavior is determined by a combination of cognitive factors, the environment, and stimuli

noncount noun

demonstrative pronouns

parallel teaching

noun that cannot be counted and thus cannot be changed into a plural form

point out or draw attention to something or someone (*This is my apartment.*)

content area and ESL teachers teach their respective groups at the same time; they may, at times, switch groups in this scenario

proper noun

Basic Inventory of Natural Language (BINL)

participial phrase

the name of a specific person, place, or thing

used to measure oral-language proficiency in one of thirty-two different languages by asking students to describe a set of images

a verbal phrase that acts as an adjective

simple sentence

adjective

integrative framework

has only one independent clause and no dependent clauses

word that describes or modifies a noun or a pronoun

a plan for achieving goals in all subject areas by combining content across disciplines

acquisition-learning hypothesis

morphology

equal access

one of the five hypotheses of the monitor model; learning the rules of a language will not allow users to produce output; only authentic acquisition will allow students to use their new language effectively

the study of word forms and their component parts

provides procedural safeguards to ensure that all students receive the same benefits of public education regardless of disabilities

silent period

Erik Erikson

active voice

time at the beginning of second-language acquisition when students are either unwilling or unable to communicate in their new language

a researcher who developed a theory of psychosocial development that focuses on reconciling individual needs with the needs of society through stages

a sentence construction in which the subject of the sentence performs the main action of the sentence

prepositional phrase

semantics

regional and social dialects

a phrase that begins with a preposition and ends with an object of the preposition

the study of meaning in language

language variations that are common to the people in a certain region or social group

indefinite pronouns

Albert Bandura

attribution theory

refers to a nonspecific thing or things (*Someone has to know the answer.*)

a Canadian psychologist who developed the social learning theory

internal attribution is assumed when other people make mistakes or are victims, as individuals tend to see others as a predictable stereotype; when an individual makes a mistake, he or she tends to view the cause as external

IDEA Proficiency Tests (IPT)

John Dewey

honeymoon stage

designed to measure the oral proficiency and reading and writing abilities of K – 12 students; measure content such as vocabulary, syntax, and reading for understanding and are available in both English and Spanish

a pragmatic philosopher who viewed learning as a series of scientific inquiry and experimentation; he advocated real-world experiences and volunteerism

stage of acculturation; students are delighted about the novelty of the new culture around them

direct method

station teaching

semi-authentic materials

the principle that second languages should be acquired in much the same way as first languages; also called the natural method

students move through various stations set up in the classroom, and teachers work with them in small groups

materials based on original materials that have been adapted to fit the lesson objectives and the needs of students

Castañeda v. Pickard

vowel reduction

compound sentence

A 1981 case in which it was decided that ELL programs must meet three different requirements: 1) the program must be based on sound academic theory; 2) it must have adequate resources and personnel to implement it; and 3) the program must conduct evaluation to determine if the language barriers of students are being overcome.

the shortening or diminishing of a vowel sound

has two or more independent clauses and no dependent clauses

stem/root

consonant cluster

phonics/skills-based approach

a base word, often a free morpheme, to which other morphemes can be added

a group of two or more consonants

focuses on transferring students' literacy skills independently; in this approach, specific skills in reading, writing, and speaking are targeted and practiced each day

parentheses

Socratic Method

diphthong

punctuation marks that enclose insignificant information

a teaching technique in which a leader prompts discussion solely by asking questions and allowing the class to share and then respond to and build upon one another's ideas

the sound made when one vowel sound blends into another vowel sound in one syllable

cognitive dissonance theory

pragmatics

conjugation

uneasiness that is felt when an individual has conflicting thoughts

the study of the meaning of language in context

the process of changing the spelling of a verb and/or adding helping verbs

count noun

Migrant Education Program (MEP)

learning contract

noun that can be put into plural form

a provision of the NCLB that provided for the expansion and regulation of education programs for migrant students

agreement negotiated between a student and a teacher, with possible input from other school personnel or parents, designed for the improvement of an objective

zone of proximal development (ZPD)

predicate

monitor model

the space between what a child can do independently and the learning goal

describes what the subject is doing or being; it contains the verb(s) and any modifiers or objects that accompany it/them

a set of five hypotheses developed by researcher Stephen Krashen; according to Krashen, there is no fundamental difference in the way that humans acquire first and subsequent languages

verbal phrase

Jean Piaget

self-assessment

a phrase that begins with a word that would normally act as a verb but is instead filling another role within the sentence

a Swiss psychologist who was the first to study cognition in children; identified stages of development and contributed to schema learning

a method by which students monitor their own progress toward learning goals

sociolinguistic competence

Jerome Bruner

phonology

using language in a socially appropriate way and understanding register

a constructivist theorist who contributed the three modes of representation to the field of cognitive development

the study of the sounds and patterns of particular languages

nasalization

comprehensible input

denotation

sound produced when air comes through the nose (*n*)

language that is just slightly above the student's current grasp; new information that students are able to understand because it is introduced alongside information they already know

a word's dictionary definition

early multiword stage

question mark

colons

stage of language acquisition; children begin using elements of grammar and repeating longer sentences, though they are still unable to create their own

used to end questions

used to let a reader know a list or explanation is upcoming in the sentence

communicative language teaching

pull-out programs

overextend

focuses on students' abilities to communicate through interactions in the target language; in CLT instruction, students use authentic texts and realistic scenarios to practice skills they would use outside the classroom

certified ESOL teachers take small groups of students from their content area classrooms for limited portions of the school day to receive specialized instruction focusing on intensive vocabulary and grammar objectives

when a child's definition of a word is too broad

transcription

language acquisition

short-term memory

way to visually represent sounds

a subconscious process in which language is internalized without deliberate intent

information that enters the conscious memory but is not stored for recall at a later time

transitional stage

one-on-one

fossilization

stage of literacy development; characterized by a steady reading pace and an understanding of multiple strategies that can be used to decode difficult texts

a type of instruction in which a teacher works with one individual student on a concept

the point in second-language acquisition in which a learner's growth freezes in place and further linguistic development becomes highly unlikely

usage

linguistic determinism

formal operational stage

the generally accepted ways in which words and phrases are used in different contexts

the belief that all human thought and action is controlled by language

final stage of Piaget's cognitive-developmental theory; eleven years of age and older; adolescents in this stage demonstrate intelligence through logical use of symbols and their relationship to abstract concepts

later multiword stage

interference (negative transfer)

ACCESS

stage of language acquisition; children average four to six words per sentence and can learn as many as twenty words per day

when language learners incorrectly apply the rules of their native language to the language they are learning

Accessing Comprehension and Communication in English State-to-State; large-scale progress-monitoring assessment

motor disabilities

Benjamin Bloom

operant conditioning

characterized by loss of movement; may be caused by injury or disease

contributed to the taxonomy of educational objectives and the theory of mastery learning

provides rewards or punishment as a motivation for desired performance

Bilingual Syntax Measure (BSM) I and II

bias

grammar

measure oral proficiency in English and/or Spanish and must be administered individually; student scores are based on the grammatical structures of their oral responses

favoring something over another, often unreasonably

the set of rules that apply to properly structured sentences

linguistic competence

grammar-translation method

noun phrase

knowledge of the linguistic components of a language such as morphology, syntax, and semantics

instructors help students recognize similarities between their native and learned languages by teaching in students' native languages and concentrating on grammatical rules of a target language

consists of a noun and its modifiers

intransitive verb

direct object

creole

verb that does not require a direct object

a noun that receives the action of the verb

a pidgin language that becomes nativized, meaning people begin speaking it as a first language

affective-filter hypothesis

language learning

self-motivation

one of the five hypotheses of the monitor model; stressors such as low self-esteem, poor motivation, and anxiety may all inhibit language acquisition

comes through direct instruction: students are conscious of the fact that they are learning and are able to speak about their new knowledge and explain where it comes from

the drive from within that inspires a person to work toward something

learning theories

elision

think-pair-share

describe how genetics, development, environment, motivation, and emotions affect a student's ability to acquire and apply knowledge

when sounds are omitted from the pronunciation of a word, usually because the omission makes the words easier to use in everyday speech

when students reflect on a question individually and then turn to other students nearby to share and discuss their responses

stress

International Phonetic Alphabet (IPA)

babbling stage

emphasis placed on syllables or words

a notation used to represent the phonemes used in spoken language

stage of language acquisition; infants usually play by controlling the pitch and volume of their vocalizations and learn to produce sounds based on friction